Presented by the
Walsall Action Group

Jesus grew angry.
He shook his head.
"No," He said,
*"don't send these
children away.
Let them come to Me!
The kingdom of heaven
belongs to anyone who
is as trusting and
willing as these
children."*

BRITISH & FOREIGN
BIBLE
SOCIETY

Adventure Story Bible

Book 7

Trusting God

Written by Anne de Graaf

Illustrated by José Pérez Montero

Bible Society

Trusting God

Contents — Ruth; Job; 1 Samuel 1–2

Book 7 — Bible background

The Book of Ruth is a story which shows how much God cares for people. He cared enough to help two women, Naomi and Ruth, through the problems of everyday life.

God loved each person in Israel, as well as whole tribes. Although the tribes of Israel often forgot the Lord's laws there were men and women who lived good lives, and who prayed to God and worshipped him.

The Book of Ruth tells about a girl called Ruth who was not a member of God's people Israel, yet chose to follow her mother-in—law Naomi and trust the one, true God. In making that choice Ruth freed herself to be used by God and became a member of the people of Israel. It was into the family of Ruth that Jesus was eventually born.

The Book of Job is about a man who held on to his faith in God despite all the bad things which happened to him. Job knew that God does not cause pain and suffering. His friends thought Job's suffering was sent by God, but they were wrong.

The Book of Job explores areas of life which are difficult to understand, such as why there is evil and suffering in the world. Through Job we can learn that the Lord is in control, no matter how desperate things may seem.

The 1st Book of Samuel tells about the time in Israel's history before they had kings. It tells the story of Samuel, who was born in answer to his mother's prayers. His mother Hannah had to wait a long time before she was able to have children, but in turning to God her faith and trust became deeper. Samuel grew up to become the first great prophet in Israel. He warned his people about what would happen if they did not stop turning away from God and doing wrong.

Samuel listened to God and warned the people of Israel that they should follow God's laws. Through Samuel God was to choose the first king of Israel, Saul, and later choose David to become Israel's greatest king.

GOD CARES FOR RUTH

A bad time

Ruth 1.1–13

Many people in Israel were ignoring God's laws at this time, but some people remembered to teach their children to love God. They lived in the way that God wanted, obeying the laws God had given to Moses.

One such person was a woman called Naomi. She was married and had two sons whom she loved very much. Because there was a famine where they lived — a time when there wasn't much food — the family moved away from where the other tribes of Israel were living. Then her husband died and Naomi was very sad.

Naomi brought up her boys well, teaching them about the Lord. When they grew up, her sons married. The girls they married were not people of Israel but belonged instead to the Moabite tribe, who had been enemies of Israel for many years. Yet Naomi loved these girls as if they were her own daughters.

Then the two sons died and Naomi and the two young wives were left alone. It was a very sad time for the three women as they missed their husbands very much. The wives were called Orpah and Ruth. They lived with Naomi, helping her as much as they could.

Some time later Naomi heard that the famine in Judah, her home, was over. God had given them a good harvest. So Naomi decided it was time to return home with her daughters-in-law. They were on their way when Naomi said, "My daughters, my people were one of the tribes of Israel and it is right that I go back there now But it would be better for you to go back to your own parents. They will take care of you and perhaps you will even find husbands again."

Naomi was very upset because her sons were dead, and to send away their wives would be like losing her daughters as well.

The young women said, "No, no, we will stay with you."

But Naomi would not hear of it. "What will you do? I am too old to find another husband. And even if I could, would you wait twenty years until any sons I had were old enough to marry you? Don't be silly. Go back home where you can find some men to care for you." Naomi wanted the best for her daughters-in-law.

Ruth stands by Naomi

Ruth 1.14–22

The two young women loved their mother-in-law very much. She had been like a mother to them both. "Please, will you let us stay with you?" they asked.

"No, go back to your families," Naomi said. She wished they would go away quickly. She loved them so much it was very hard to tell them to go.

Naomi felt a hand on her shoulder. It was Orpah. "I will do what you wish and go back to my parents," she said. Naomi hugged her and they cried together, knowing that they

would never see each other again. Orpah gathered her things and left.

When Orpah had gone Naomi said, "Your sister-in-law has gone back to her family, and you should do the same." But Ruth did not want to leave Naomi, and answered, "Please don't ask me to leave you! Let me go with you.

"I will go where you go. Your people will be my people and your God, my God." Ruth knew about the one, true God, even though she was not an Israelite. Her husband, Naomi's son, had taught her about God and she trusted him. "Please, Naomi," Ruth begged. "I never want to be far away from you. God will take care of us."

means 'Pleasant.' Call me Mara, which means 'Bitter.' The Lord has taken so much away from me, I am bitter now."

Ruth said nothing, although she still felt very sad about her husband's death. She held Naomi's hand and hoped she would be able to help Naomi get over her bitterness.

Ruth goes to work

Ruth 2.1–22

The barley harvest was just beginning when Naomi and Ruth arrived in Bethlehem, and Ruth decided to go and find food. "I'll go out into the fields and see if there is any barley left over, then bring it home," she said to Naomi. "I'm sure to find someone who will let me work with him." Naomi nodded. "You do that, my daughter," she said.

It was part of Hebrew law that when taking in the harvest the reapers should leave some for the poor to collect. This was one of the laws God had given to the Israelites to make sure that everyone had enough to eat, and that people shared and cared for each other.

It so happened that Ruth went to a field owned by a rich man called Boaz. Boaz was from Bethlehem, just like Naomi. In fact, they were part of the same family. When Boaz came to the field to watch the workers, he saw Ruth and asked a servant who she was.

Boaz was a good man who loved and thanked God for the many ways in which God provided for him. When the servant told Boaz who Ruth was, and how loyal she was to Naomi, he wanted to help. He called her to him.

"Please, sir," Ruth said, "may I pick up any barley which your servants leave behind?"

"Certainly, certainly," Boaz said. "I've heard how good you have been to your mother-in-law and I'll help you in any way I can. Work in this field with the women here, and stay with them. When you are thirsty, you can drink from their water jars."

When Naomi saw how determined Ruth was, she held out her arms, and the girl came and hugged her. They would stay together.

Naomi and Ruth set out for Bethlehem, where Naomi had grown up. When they arrived all the elder people remembered Naomi.

Old friends hugged her and the word soon spread, "Naomi has come back home and she has brought her daughter-in-law with her!"

But all Naomi could think of was how happy she had been when she left Bethlehem as a young bride. Now she was returning, but without her husband and sons. She felt sorry for herself.

"Don't call me Naomi," she said. "That

"You are so kind to me," Ruth said. "Even though I'm not equal to your servants you have cared for me and made me feel better."

When it was time to eat, Boaz asked Ruth to join him and the other workers. After the meal Ruth still had some food left, so she saved it to take home for Naomi. Then she went back into the fields, and Boaz turned to his workers. "Let Ruth pick up the corn even where the bundles are lying," he said, "and leave some specially for her."

The workers did what Boaz said and by the end of the day Ruth had gathered a full basket of barley. That was more than enough for her and Naomi. She brought the basket home that evening, together with the food she had saved from the meal.

"Ruth!" Naomi said, "where did you find so much food?"

"Oh Naomi, I met a man who was so kind and good," Ruth said. "His name is Boaz. He helped me and said I can come and gather left-over corn in his fields whenever I want to."

Then for the first time in many months Naomi felt happier, and smiled. "Ruth," Naomi said, "Boaz is a member of my family. He is my relative, and if he is taking care of us then all should be well."

The two women sat down to eat and thanked God for taking such good care of them.

The great-grandmother of a king

Ruth 2.23—4.22

For the rest of the barley harvest Ruth worked hard in Boaz's fields. She always came home with more food than she needed, and Boaz continued to be kind to her.

One day near the end of the harvest Naomi said to Ruth, "Ruth, you're young and you need a home of your own. We need to find you a husband. I have a plan. Now do what I tell you."

It was the custom in those days, when a woman had lost her husband, for her nearest relative to marry her. Boaz was the nearest relative of Ruth, and Naomi could see that he cared for her.

So Ruth agreed to Naomi's plan. That evening Ruth got out her best clothes. She washed, put on her best perfume, and got ready. Naomi thought Ruth looked beautiful, and sent her off to see Boaz.

Boaz had worked outside that night and he was sleeping under the stars. Ruth crept up to him and lay down at his feet. In the middle of the night he woke up with a start. "Who's there, sleeping by my feet?" he whispered in the dark. "It's me, Ruth. Because you are a close relative, you are responsible for taking care of

me. I've come to ask if you would take me as your wife. You have always been so good to me."

Boaz sat up. "Ruth," he said, "you are so lovely. Any man would be honoured to make you his wife. It's true that I am a close relative, but there is a man who is a closer relative to you than I am. I'll see him tomorrow. If he will take responsibility for you, well and good. If not, then I will. Meanwhile lie down and stay here until the morning."

The next morning Ruth went home to Naomi and told her all that had happened. She took barley home as a present from Boaz. Naomi was pleased with how things had gone. "I'm sure you will hear from Boaz today," she said.

Meanwhile Boaz went to see the closer relative of Ruth, and they agreed that Boaz would look after Ruth. When Naomi and Ruth heard this they were overjoyed. They let all their friends know the good news — there was going to be a wedding! The wedding was a very special day, and Ruth's happiness was made complete in seeing Naomi happy once again.

As the years went by Boaz and Ruth grew to love each other very much and they had a baby boy. They called him Obed. Naomi loved her new grandson, and took care of him.

When Naomi was holding the baby on her lap one day all her old friends came by and said, "Naomi is smiling again. Ruth was better to her than seven sons. See how the Lord has blessed them!"

Many years later David, the great king of Israel, was born into Obed's family. So Ruth and Boaz, because of their loyalty and kindness, were blessed by God and became the great-grandparents of a mighty king!

WHY DOES A GOOD MAN SUFFER?

In heaven

Job 1.1–12

God was ruling in heaven, listening to what his angels told him about all that was happening on earth. God tried to help people whenever they let him. If they obeyed his laws, God blessed them.

Satan was among the heavenly beings, and God asked him, "What have you been doing?" Satan said, "I've been around the earth, roaming here and there."

"Have you seen my man Job?" God said. "He is so good, always trying to please me and do what is right. He prays to me and listens when I answer his prayers."

Satan nodded. He had indeed seen Job. "Job is only good because he knows you will be good to him," he said. "Look at all the sheep and cattle you have given him. Look how healthy his family is. You think Job loves you? Ha! He just cares about becoming rich."

God knew this was not true. Job obeyed God because he loved him.

"You protect Job too much," Satan said. "Suppose you take away everything he has. Then we'll see if he really loves you or not."

God already knew how much Job loved him. Job was a man who walked with God all the days of his life, whatever happened. God loved Job very much.

"All right," God said. "Everything he has is in your power, but you mustn't hurt Job himself."

Abandoned by everyone but God

Job 1.13–22

There are bad days, and there are very bad days. After God said it was all right for Satan to test Job, Job had a very, very bad day. Everything that could go wrong, did go wrong. Job could not see the reason behind his suffering, but throughout it all he knew one thing for sure. God loved him, and he trusted God. That was enough.

That terrible day started when Job's children were having a big party. A servant came running up to Job.

"Tragedy has struck!" he said. "A band of enemies came and killed all your oxen and donkeys, as well as the servants in the field. I was the only one to escape!"

No sooner had the servant finished telling his story, when another servant arrived, panting. "Oh, Job, it's terrible! I was in the pasture with all your sheep when lightning struck them and your shepherds, and killed them all. I am the only one who escaped to tell you."

"My story is even worse," another servant said, out of breath from running so fast. "Oh, Job, another band of enemies came and stole all your camels, killing all the servants except for me!"

Job looked from one servant to the other. How could so much go wrong in one day? But then the worst news of all arrived.

"Job, Job!" It was one of the servants from
his eldest son's house. "A great wind came
and blew the house down where all your
children were having their party. They are all
dead!" the servant said.

At this Job was so upset he tore his clothes
and shaved his head. Then he fell to the
ground and prayed. "Lord, I had nothing when
I was born. All the sheep, camels, donkeys,
oxen, and crops were gifts you gave me. Even
my children were your blessings. If you
choose to take them away from me, I accept
that. I know you are wise and almighty, and I
bless you!"

This was not what Satan had expected from
Job. He thought that Job would have blamed
God. God looked down at Job and was
pleased with him.

In the court of heaven Satan said, "It's not enough that I destroyed his property and his family. Let me hurt his body and make him ill. Then you will see how much he really loves you! It's one thing losing your possessions, but another thing to be ill and in pain."

Once again, the Lord let Satan test Job, but he told him that he must not kill Job.

Satan went back to earth and made Job become very ill. Red sores covered his skin. Job's wife could hardly look at him. "What is wrong with you?" she shouted. "How can you still trust in God after all that's happened?"

But Job still didn't say anything against God, and kept on trusting him.

LIFE CAN BE BITTER

Moaning and groaning

Job 2.11–3.26

Job had three good friends called Eliphaz, Bildad, and Zophar. News of all Job's problems soon reached them. They were very upset that so many bad things could happen to their friend all at once. Eliphaz, Bildad, and Zophar packed up their camels and set off to visit their friend, Job. "Maybe we can help poor Job," they said to each other.

When they came to Job's fields they saw that the crops had gone. Job's pastures were full of dead sheep and cattle. They saw the house which blew down on top of Job's children. They shook their heads at how terrible it all was.

When they reached Job's house they saw someone in the distance, sitting in the dirt. He was covered with ugly, red sores and could not stop scratching himself.

"Sir," the friends asked the man sitting on the ground. "Could you tell us where the owner of this house is? We want to help him. Please, do you know where Job is?"

Job looked up at the men on their camels. He squinted into the sun. "Don't you know me?" he whispered.

Eliphaz climbed off his camel and came closer. "I'm sorry, sir. I couldn't hear you. We're looking for our friend Job. Do you know where he is?"

Again Job said, "Don't you know me?"

Eliphaz stooped down. "Oh no! This is Job!" he said. He hugged his poor friend who had lost so much and who was so ill. All the friends cried with Job and tore their clothes with grief.

When they saw there was nothing they could do, the three friends sat down with Job and held his hands so Job wouldn't feel so alone. Job's friends sat in the dirt keeping him company for seven days and nights. They said nothing because there were no words to describe how sorry they felt for him.

Finally, after seven days, Job spoke. "I don't understand why all this has happened!" he said.

Job didn't know it was Satan who had caused him to suffer so much. He cried out, "I don't know why life has become so terrible!" Job even wished for death. He moaned and groaned until he thought his heart would break. But Job still didn't blame God or become angry with him, which is what Satan had thought would happen.

The reason why

Job 4.1—5.27

After Job had broken the silence and cried out that he wished he could die, his friend Eliphaz talked for a long time. He tried to explain why Job might have run into so much trouble.

Eliphaz said, "Job, there must be a good reason for all this. Let's just think for a moment. No one is perfect, and God purifies us in order to help us.

"Job," Eliphaz continued, "you know that people do fall on hard times. You have often helped other people out when they've been in trouble. So maybe now it is your turn to get in trouble. It can happen to anybody, you know."

Job said nothing. He listened to his friend's

reasoning, but he knew deep down that this was not the answer to his troubles.

Eliphaz went on, "Job, you must accept what God is doing to you, and not fight against it. God will correct you and then make things better. It's as simple as that!"

But it wasn't that simple, and Job knew it.

Is Job guilty?

Job 8.1–22, 11.1–20, 15.1–35, 18.1–21, 20.1–29, 22.1–30, 25.1–6, 32.1–36.33

Job's friends grew angry with him for saying that he had done nothing wrong. They wanted him to say he was sorry, and he wouldn't. But although Job asked God why all this trouble was happening to him, he didn't blame God. Job had faith in himself. He had done nothing wrong, but his friends didn't understand.

"Job," Bildad said, "you were a good man. I'm sure if you just say you're sorry for something and beg God to forgive you, he will bless you again."

Zophar said, "Job, you're making fun of God by saying you've done nothing wrong. You must have done something terrible, or none of this would be happening! Why are you saying you've done nothing wrong? Everybody does something wrong. Think, man, think!"

Eliphaz and Bildad picked up where Zophar left off. They had become so angry with Job that they forgot the pain Job was in. Instead of speaking gently and helping Job they called him names and made him feel even worse.

"Job, there's no reason to think you are a good man!"

"Give up, and admit what you did wrong!"

All three of them said to Job, "You talk too much, you old windbag! Look! God is punishing you for all the bad things you've done!

"You say God is not teaching you a lesson, but we know he is. Admit it!" they said.

The three friends huffed and puffed at poor old Job. They tried in every way they knew to make him admit he was bad and that God was punishing him. But Job kept shaking his head. He knew that he had done nothing wrong. Eventually they ran out of arguments and were quiet.

But a young man, Elihu, who had been standing nearby listening to them talking, would not believe Job was right. He was angry with Job's friends for not arguing more with Job. Elihu said, "Job, God rules over all. He has made you suffer to teach you a lesson. You are too proud! Do you think God will listen to someone like you? Ha!"

But Job knew that he had done nothing wrong. That's why, whatever his friends said, he knew without a doubt that God was not punishing him. He couldn't understand why he was suffering, or why God didn't seem to be answering his questions. But he continued to ask God, and didn't blame him. His friends had given him the same old answers to his troubles, but Job wanted to know from God himself.

WHERE IS GOD?
Job tries to find God

Job 6.1–7.21, 9.1–10.22, 12.1–14.22, 16.1–17.16, 19.1–29, 21.1–34, 23.1–24.25, 26.1–31.40

As Job listened to his friends giving him so much advice, he knew they could not comfort him. "All your words only upset me," Job said. "They hurt me more than any illness. I needed loyal friends.

"My God!" Job shouted. "You seem so far away from me now. If only I could be with you!" His friends kept arguing with him, but Job had had enough. He didn't want to listen any more. "Lord," he said, "you are the only one who can answer me. I want to be at your side!" Job shouted again.

Zophar said to Bildad, "He makes it so hard on himself. If only he would admit to doing wrong."

Job swung round and looked at Zophar as though he were an enemy. "No, Zophar, you are wrong. People who do wrong are not always punished, and it is not only evil people who suffer."

Often people who suffer are poor people, or children who have no parents to take care of them; people who are homeless or living in a country where there is war.

"It's not because they have done anything wrong that they suffer," Job said, "and it's not God's fault that these things happen. There's another reason, but I don't know what it is.

"Who knows more than God?" Job said. "He knows the answers. But you," he pointed at the men, "you know nothing. Your answers are as empty as the wind."

19

God speaks

Job 38.1—39.30

Job's friends heard Job, but they didn't understand him. They thought he *must* have done something wrong.

But God had been watching and listening to all Job and his friends said. Job had not blamed God for what had happened. He may not have understood what was happening but he knew that his suffering could not be punishment from God, and he knew that justice would be done.

The time had come for God to answer. But God did not start by answering all the questions the men had been asking.

God helped Job to understand him by asking him questions. It was the Lord's turn to ask, and Job's turn to try and find the answers.

"Where were you when I made the earth?" God asked. "Can you even measure the earth?

"Who made the stars and listened to them sing? Who keeps the sea from covering all the land? Have you ever told the sun when to rise, or walked on the bottom of the ocean?

20

Where does light come from and why is there darkness?"

The more questions God asked, the more Job realized he did not know. His picture of himself changed. "I am a man who hardly knows right from wrong," he thought to himself.

God asked, "Do you know how to make rain or hail or snow? Can you cause the cold to turn water into ice? Who tells the stars which way to go?

"Think about the animals I have made. Do you find food for lions to eat? Do you know why wild donkeys are free?

"Why does an ostrich run so fast? And how does the eagle soar so high in the sky? Do you know any of these things?"

"I do not know the answers to any of these questions," Job thought to himself. "I know so little and God knows so much. He is far greater than I ever imagined. What can I say?"

DO ALL QUESTIONS NEED TO BE ANSWERED?

The creator

Job 40.1–41.34

"Lord, I spoke foolishly," Job said. "I don't even know how to start answering your questions. I have nothing to say, Lord. I have already said more than I should."

"Ah, but Job," God said, "are you trying to prove that I am unjust? That I am wrong and you are right? I created the strongest of all the animals, and I created you.

"I created crocodiles," God said. "Can you even catch a crocodile? What would you use — a hook and bait on a fishing rod? I made him as strong and powerful as he is, but you cannot even touch him. Do you have the same power as me?"

Job shook his head. There was so much he did not know. Job thought about all that God had said.

Starting again

Job 42.1–17

Job had seen God as the creator of the moon and the earth, the one who breathes the wind, and the sculptor of flowers.

Job knew God had not given him exact answers to his questions. Instead, God had given him much more. God had cared enough about Job to come to him and talk to him. Job would know that what he thought and what had happened to him mattered to God. The God who created heaven and earth wanted to meet Job and help him understand who he was.

Job was willing to trust that God hates sadness and suffering even more than he did. God is great and good. He cares about us and wants us to know him. That was enough for Job.

"You can do everything," Job said to the Lord. "You have talked about things too great for me to understand. You have taught me this with your questions. I have listened and learned. I have heard and believed. In the past I only knew what others had told me. Now I see you, both in my mind and heart.

"Lord, I am sorry for saying foolish things. Please forgive me. I am only a man who loves you."

Job poured out his heart to God, and worshipped him.

But God was not happy with Job's friends. They had not spoken the truth about God, as Job had. God told them, "Job will pray for you, and then I will forgive you."

So despite all the added pain his friends had caused him, Job prayed for them. In doing this Job forgave his friends and God answered Job's prayer and forgave them, too.

After Job had prayed for his friends God made him prosperous again. Each of Job's relatives and friends came and gave him presents. Job started again.

Because Job knew what it meant to suffer he became wise and was able to comfort many people who were in trouble. God blessed him, and Job lived a long life and had seven little boys. His three daughters became the loveliest in the land. Job lived so long that he was even able to play with his grandchildren's children.

Job had experienced great suffering and pain, but he knew that God loved him and wanted him to be honest about how he felt.

HANNAH'S WISH COMES TRUE

Waiting for a baby

1 Samuel 1.1–5

The people of Israel were God's special people, but sometimes they forgot about him. Then something would happen to bring them back to God.

During the time when the people of Israel had no king they again chose to forget God. Most people did not even try to do what God wanted. At this time there lived a man named Elkanah. Elkanah had two wives, as people sometimes did in those days. One had children, and the other had none.

Elkanah's wife who had no children was called Hannah. She had long black hair and dark eyes which lit up when she smiled. Elkanah loved Hannah very much. He liked nothing better than to make Hannah smile and laugh.

But as the years went by and Hannah still didn't have any children, she smiled less and less often. Hannah and Elkanah waited and prayed, hoping all the time that they might have a child.

Elkanah's other wife was called Peninnah. Peninnah had given Elkanah many sons and daughters but she teased Hannah and made fun of her, telling her that she was a useless wife because she could not give Elkanah even one child.

Elkanah was one of the few people at that time who tried to follow the Lord. Once a year he took the whole family to Shiloh. There the Lord's Covenant Box containing the Ten Commandments was kept in a holy tent. A priest took care of the Covenant Box and made offerings at an altar there.

Peninnah hurts Hannah

1 Samuel 1.6-9

One year, after Elkanah had finished worshipping God at Shiloh, all his family were having a meal together. Hannah was there, and Peninnah and her children.

Hannah felt sad as she saw Peninnah with all her children. It made it even worse when Peninnah started teasing her. Each year Hannah tried not to listen to the insults of Peninnah and her children, but as time went by and she still had no baby they became harder and harder to ignore.

This time Peninnah's teasing was more cruel than usual. "You're getting old, Hannah. Look at all my children. You don't have any. What will you do when you are really old and don't have any children to care for you?"

Hannah could not take it any more. She burst into tears and covered her face. She wanted a baby so much. "Why, oh why don't I have a child?" she cried out in her heart.

Elkanah saw Hannah crying. He had not heard what Peninnah had said, but he guessed. Peninnah was always saying spiteful things to Hannah that made her cry. Elkanah said, "Hannah, why are you crying? It is not so bad, really. Don't be upset about not having a child. It's all right. Look, our love is so special, don't I mean more to you than ten sons?"

Elkanah didn't know that Hannah's longing for a baby was not something which would go away because she loved Elkanah. Her love for Elkanah was not any less because she wanted a child. "But it's not all right!" Hannah thought. She stood up and left the table.

When he saw her leave, Elkanah thought to himself, "She will get over it in time."

A prayer from the heart

1 Samuel 1.10–18

Hannah walked away from the family
gathering towards the altar where offerings
were made to God. Her heart was heavy. She
wanted a baby so much, but there was
nothing more she could do.

Hannah started praying silently to the Lord.
She was so unbearably sad that she couldn't
put it into words. Her lips moved as she
prayed. The tears streamed down her face as
the bitterness she felt overflowed out of her
heart.

"O Lord," she prayed quietly, "I want a
baby so badly. Please, God. If you would give
me a son I would dedicate him to you and
bring him back here to be brought up by your
priest. The child would be yours from the
beginning. Please God, hear my prayer."

While Hannah was praying Eli the priest sat
nearby, watching her. Eli saw her lips move,
but heard no sound. Hannah's eyes were red
from crying.

In those days there were not many people
in Israel who went to Eli's tent to pray and
those who did prayed out loud. Some people
who had come to Shiloh to celebrate even
entered the tent while they were drunk. So
when the priest saw Hannah's red eyes and
saw her lips move but no sound come
out, he thought she had had too
much to drink.

"You there!" he said. "This is not
the place for you to come if you are
drunk."

"No, sir," Hannah cried, "please don't think
I'm one of those drunken people who stumble
in here during the feast! I am a woman who is
very sad. I have not been drinking. I was
pouring out my troubles to God."

As Eli came closer to Hannah he could see
how unhappy she was. He knew she spoke
the truth. "Go in peace," he said, "and may
the God of Israel give you what you have
asked of him."

Hannah bowed her head. "Thank you for your blessing, sir," she said. As Hannah walked away she felt the weight of worry and shame lift from her heart. By the time Hannah reached Elkanah, she was smiling again.

Baby Samuel

1 Samuel 1.19–25

The next morning Elkanah and his family returned home. Elkanah was so pleased to see Hannah looking happier.

Soon Hannah became pregnant and gave birth to a boy, whom she named Samuel.

Hannah said she gave her son that name because she asked the Lord for him and he heard her. The name "Samuel" was related to the Hebrew word "ask." Hannah and Elkanah were overjoyed that the Lord had answered their prayers.

While Samuel was young, Elkanah continued going up to Shiloh once a year to worship God. Hannah decided not to go with him. When Samuel was a little older she would take him there to live with the priest and then he would be dedicated to the Lord as she had promised.

When Samuel was three, Hannah knew that the time had come to join the family on the

yearly journey to Shiloh, and take Samuel to Eli, the priest. Hannah had never forgotten the promise she made to God. Samuel had been a gift from God to start with. Handing him over to Eli so he would grow closer to God was continuing the step she took on that day when Eli thought she was drunk. She had trusted God with her prayer for a child, and now she was trusting God to take care of her son.

Hannah leaves Samuel with Eli

1 Samuel 1.26–2.11

Elkanah and Hannah took Samuel to Eli. Hannah held Samuel's hand tightly in her own. They stood at the door of the tent in Shiloh where the Lord was worshipped.

"Eli!" Hannah called out. When the old man appeared, Hannah said, "Remember me? I am the woman whose prayers you blessed. I was praying for a baby, and look how the Lord has answered my prayers." She smiled down at Samuel.

Hannah had had a long talk with Samuel, telling him how he would belong to God in a special way. He knew the priest Eli would take care of him now. And even if he was not too sure what that meant, Samuel was not afraid. His mother and father had told him God would take care of him wherever he was. Samuel trusted them and he trusted the Lord. He knew he would see his parents when the family came to Shiloh every year.

"I promised this child to God when I prayed here," Hannah continued, "and now he is old enough for you to take care of him."

Eli nodded. He slowly bent down until he was looking Samuel in the eye. "Welcome, friend," he said.

Adventure Story Bible
Old Testament